A Primer for Teachers and Leaders

A Primer for Teachers and Leaders

LEROY FORD

Illustrated by Doug Dillard

BROADMAN PRESS • Nashville, Tennessee

4234-04
ISBN: 0-8054-3404-6

Library of Congress catalog card number: 63-19069
Printed in the United States of America

This book of pictures and words is dedicated to the hundreds of thousands of volunteer teachers and leaders in the churches of our country.

It has been assembled with the hope that learning to learn and learning to teach may become pleasant and interesting experiences.

Some Questions This Book
Will Help You Answer

He is himself!

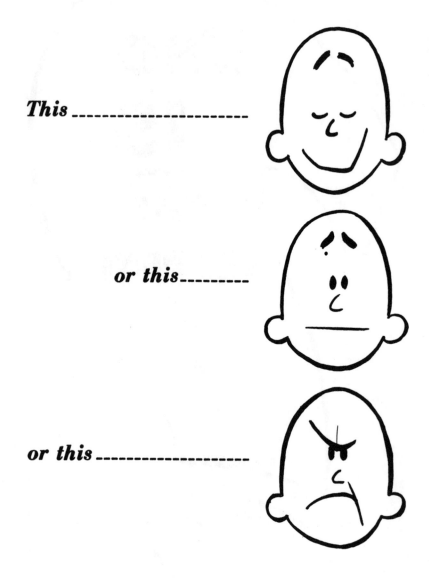

This _____

or this _____

or this _____

may be the learner.

He is different from

other persons . . .

...in background and experience....

The learner's

individual differences

affect the way

he learns.

Some Questions for You to Think About

1. What are some ways in which people differ?

   _____   _____
   _____   _____
   _____   _____
   _____   _____

2. Why do some people learn more quickly than others?

   _____
   _____
   _____

3. What do we mean when we say tnat a person is "talented"? _____

   _____
   _____

4. Who would know more about airplanes—a farmer or an airplane pilot? Why? _____

   _____
   _____
   _____

5. Who could learn to play basketball more easily—an elderly man or a teen-age boy? Why? _____

   _____
   _____
   _____

6. Who would be most apt to make the right decision about a moral problem—a person with good religious training or a person with no religious training? Why? _____

   _____

7. How do individual differences determine what and how a teacher teaches? _____

   _____
   _____

He learns through
his experiences.

Many—but not all—of the learner's experiences come through his senses.

He has five of them.

1. SIGHT

2. HEARING

3. SMELL

4. TASTE

5. TOUCH

Learning is usually better when the learner uses more than one sense at the same time.

Some experiences cannot be accounted for through the senses.

"For I did not receive it from man, nor was I taught it, but it came through a revelation of Jesus Christ."

| ... Paul

GALATIANS 1:12, RSV

There are many kinds of experiences.

Some experiences are direct ,
real life experiences .

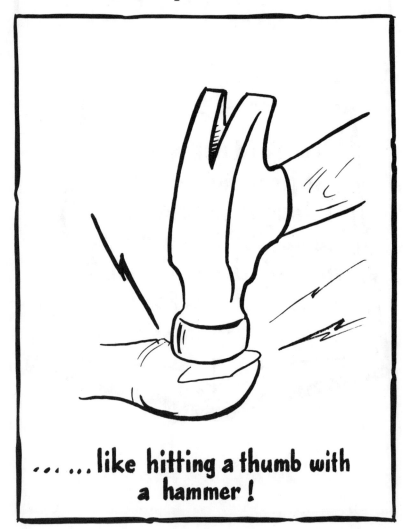

...... like hitting a thumb with
a hammer !

... or going on a trip

Some experiences are *direct*, but they are "made-up" or "play-like" experiences . . .

...like acting in a play

Some experiences are *indirect*, using representations of real things . . .

... like seeing a film

Some experiences are *indirect*, using words or symbols . . .

. . . like reading a book

... or listening to a speech

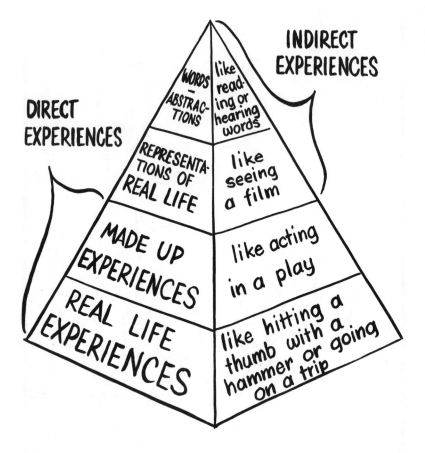

INDIRECT
EXPERIENCES

DIRECT
EXPERIENCES

WORDS — ABSTRACTIONS
like reading or hearing words

REPRESENTATIONS OF REAL LIFE
like seeing a film

MADE UP EXPERIENCES
like acting in a play

REAL LIFE EXPERIENCES
like hitting a thumb with a hammer or going on a trip

Let's picture these experiences
as a "pyramid."

This pyramid shows learning experiences arranged according to how direct or indirect they are.

● The closer to the bottom of the pyramid, the more direct the experience.

● The closer to the top of the pyramid, the more indirect the experience.

● The closer to the top of the pyramid, the fewer senses are used.

● The closer to the bottom of the pyramid, the more senses are used.

Some Questions for You to Think About

1. What is the difference between a direct experience and an indirect experience? _____
_____
_____

2. What kinds of experiences are these?
   (1) Riding a horse: _____
   (2) Riding a stick horse: _____
   (3) Looking at a picture of
       a man riding a horse: _____
   (4) Reading about a man
       who rode a horse: _____

3. What are some examples of real life experiences?
   made-up experiences? _____
   _____   _____
   _____   _____

4. List some real life experiences which adults could have in a church group on Sunday. _____
   _____   _____
   _____   _____

5. What are the five senses? _____
   _____   _____
   _____   _____

6. Name some experiences which do not come through the five senses. _____
   _____
   _____

7. What senses are used when one prays silently?
   _____
   _____

No one type of experience is always best.

The pyramid *seems* to say that only direct experiences are really good . . . .

but

OOPS!

We *almost* forgot! . . . .

Your pupil is himself!

This _____

or this _____

or this _____

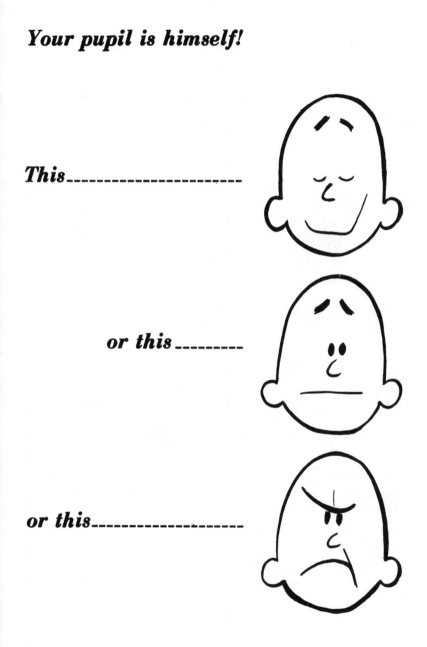

may be your pupil.

He is different from every other person . . .

The learner's differences

determine the kinds of experiences

which are best for him.

Real life experiences have advantages.

They . . .

1. Can be used with all ages
2. Help the learner learn by doing
3. Make use of several senses at the same time
4. Help the learner remember longer
5. Make learning interesting
6. Make learning natural

Real life experiences have limitations.

They . . .

1. Require a great deal of time
2. Are sometimes expensive
3. Can't be used all the time
4. Take lots of planning
5. Are difficult to use with large groups
6. Can't take place just anywhere

Made-up experiences have advantages.

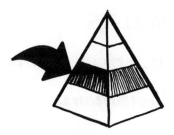

They . . .

1. Make use of several senses
2. Help the learner learn by doing
3. Are almost like real life experiences
4. Can be used with all ages
5. Can be used almost anywhere
6. Make learning interesting
7. Require participation
8. Help the learner remember longer

Made-up experiences have limitations.

They . . .

1. Take a lot of time
2. Are sometimes expensive
3. Can't be used all the time
4. Take a lot of planning
5. Are difficult to use with large groups
6. Are difficult for unskilled teachers and leaders to use

Representations
of real life
have advantages.

They . . .

1. Save time
2. Make learning uniform
3. Increase retention
4. Speed up learning
5. Make use of several senses
6. Are generally inexpensive
7. Make learning interesting
8. Can be used with groups of all sizes

Representations
of real life
have limitations.

They . . .

1. Require equipment that is sometimes hard to use
2. Are sometimes expensive
3. Cause some teachers and leaders to depend too much on the "aid"
4. Require a great deal of time if the teacher or leader prepares the aid

Abstractions (words) have advantages.

They . . .

1. Can be used to impart information quickly
2. Can be used with groups of all sizes
3. Speed up learning among persons who understand words easily
4. Are especially good for use with persons with a background of experience
5. Speed up learning by recalling experiences which are more direct
6. Can be either oral or written

Abstractions (words) have limitations.

They . . .

1. Are limited in their use with small children
2. May mean different things to different people
3. Require little active participation
4. Make use of only one sense
5. Do not build interest unless skilfully used

Some Questions for You to Think About

1. Why do Nursery-age children learn best through play?
   _____
   _____

2. Why don't babies read books? _____
   _____

3. What caused one four-year-old to call a mustache a "mouthbrow"? _____
   _____

4. Why does "cat" mean "cat" instead of "horse"?
   _____
   _____

5. Why doesn't everybody learn everything through real life experiences? _____
   _____

6. What determines which kind of experiences are best for a person? _____
   _____

7. What senses are used when one eats an orange? sees a film? takes a trip? reads a book? _____
   _____
   _____

1. Help the learner

discover what

he wants or needs

to learn.

Here are some ways . . .

Challenge him with a problem.

Ask him to write down

what he wants to learn.

Find out if the lesson fits his needs.

Ask him what his problem is.

Give him a test.

2. Use good methods.

**(but remember—no method is of itself either
effective or ineffective)**

The method depends upon

the purposes.

The method depends upon the ability of the teacher or leader.

HE WON'T DRINK!

The method depends upon
  the ability of the learner.

The method depends on

the size of the group.

The method depends on the time available.

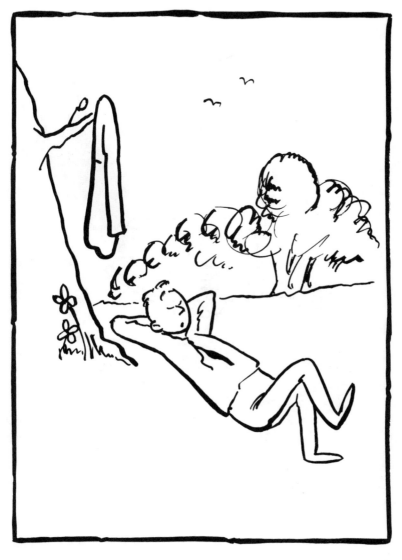

The method depends on

the facilities.

There are many

methods from which

to choose . . .

The lecture

A lecture is a speech by one speaker before an audience.

Use the lecture method . . .

1. When giving information
2. When the learners are already motivated
3. When the speaker is skilled in using word pictures
4. When the group is too large for other methods to be used
5. When adding to or stressing what the learner has read
6. When reviewing or previewing a lesson or activity
7. When pupils can understand the words used

Advantages	*Limitations*
1. Can be used with adults	1. Prevents the learner from responding
2. Conserves time	
3. Can be used with large groups	2. Few lecturers are good speakers
4. Involves use of very few aids	3. Requires that speaker know his subject
5. Can be used to add to what has been read	4. Can become uninteresting
6. Can be used to review and preview lessons or activities	5. Lecturer can take advantage of listeners
	6. Is difficult to use with children
	7. Limits retention
	8. Usually makes use of only one sense
	9. Speaker cannot always judge the reactions of the learners

The group discussion

The group discussion is a planned conversation between three or more persons on a selected topic, with leadership.

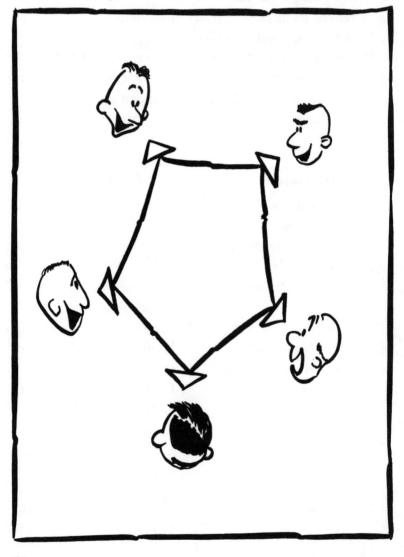

Use the group discussion method . . .

1. When sharing ideas
2. To stimulate interest in problems
3. To help members express their ideas
4. To identify and explore a problem
5. To create an informal atmosphere
6. To get opinions from persons who hesitate to speak

Advantages

1. Provides for sharing of ideas
2. Is democratic in approach
3. Encourages togetherness among members
4. Broadens viewpoints
5. Provides opportunities for sharing of leadership
6. Helps develop leadership skills

Limitations

1. Cannot be used with large groups
2. Members may have limited information
3. Discussion is easily sidetracked
4. Requires skilled leadership
5. Talkative persons may dominate conversation
6. Most people require a more formal approach

The panel

A panel is a planned conversation before an audience on a selected topic; it requires three or more panelists and a leader.

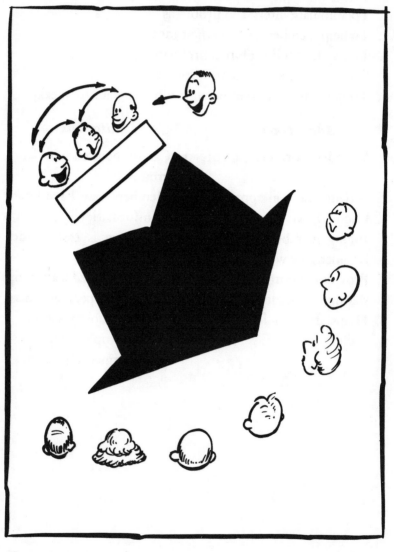

Use the panel method . . .

1. When presenting different points of view
2. When qualified panelists are available
3. When a subject is too broad to be discussed by the entire group
4. When it is best for an audience to "look in" but not respond verbally in a discussion
5. When weighing advantages and disadvantages of a solution to a problem
6. When panelists and moderator are willing to prepare

Advantages	*Limitations*
1. Stimulates thought	1. Can get sidetracked easily
2. Presents different points of view	2. Allows panelists to talk too much
3. Brings out issues	3. Does not allow all members of the group to take part
4. Stimulates analysis	
5. Makes use of best qualified persons	4. Tends to develop into a series of short speeches
	5. Divides listeners as they identify with individual panelists
	6. Requires considerable time and preparation
	7. Requires a skilled moderator

The panel-forum

A panel-forum is a panel followed by audience participation.

Use the panel-forum method . . .

1. When you want to combine content presentation and audience reaction
2. When you want group members to react to a discussion
3. When difficult ideas must be handled in the right way before they are openly questioned
4. When you have enough time
5. When weighing advantages and disadvantages of a solution to a problem
6. When you can find qualified panelists
7. When presenting different points of view

Advantages

1. Enables all group members to take part
2. Provides for a shift of responsibility
3. Allows members to react to ideas
4. Encourages purposeful listening
5. Provides a "sounding board" for views of panelists
6. Brings out issues
7. Presents different points of view

Limitations

1. Takes a lot of time
2. Requires a trained moderator
3. May seem "cut and dried" to audience
4. Allows panelists to make speeches rather than converse with each other
5. Can get sidetracked easily
6. Group members may not have skill in asking "right" questions
7. Permits talkative members to use most of forum period

Small study groups (buzz groups)

Small study groups (buzz groups) are divisions of a larger group. The groups discuss assigned problems, usually for the purpose of reporting back to the larger group.

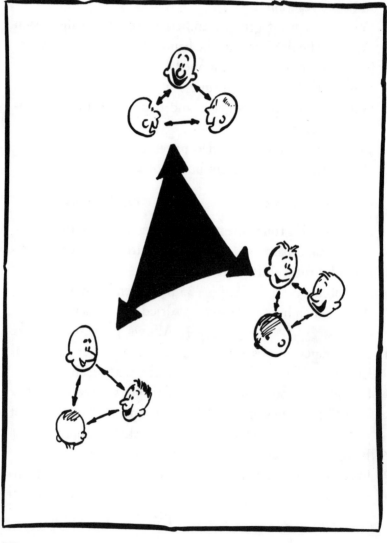

Use small study groups (buzz groups) . . .

1. When the group is too large for all members to take part
2. When exploring various facets of a subject
3. When some group members are slow to take part
4. When time is limited
5. To create a warm, friendly feeling in the group

Advantages

1. Encourages the timid members
2. Creates a warm, friendly feeling
3. Provides for sharing of leadership
4. Saves time
5. Develops leadership skills
6. Provides for pooling of ideas
7. May be used easily with other methods
8. Provides variety

Limitations

1. May result in pooling of ignorance
2. Groups may "chase rabbits"
3. Leadership may be poor
4. Reports may not be very well organized
5. Requires study beforehand if reliable conclusions are reached
6. May result in temporary cliques
7. Usually takes time to arrange equipment for use by small groups

Role playing

Role playing is the unrehearsed, dramatic enactment of a human conflict situation by two or more persons for the purpose of analysis by the group.

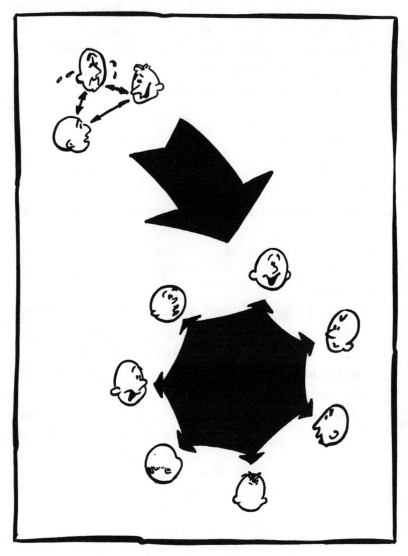

Use role playing . . .

1. When members need to increase their understanding of opposing points of view
2. When group members have ability to use the method
3. When helping members to "identify" with a problem
4. When trying to change attitudes
5. When involvement of emotions aids in presenting the problem
6. When creating the stage for problem solving

Advantages

1. Gains immediate interest
2. May be used with groups of all sizes
3. Helps members analyze situations
4. Increases self-confidence of participants
5. Helps members identify themselves with a problem
6. Helps members "experience" the other person's point of view
7. Creates the stage for problem solving

Limitations

1. Members may identify participants with the problems
2. Most members are reluctant to role play
3. Requires trained leadership
4. Limited in number of situations in which it can be used
5. Role players may have difficulty "releasing" their roles

The case study

A case study is an account of a problem situation, including sufficient detail to make it possible for groups to analyze problems involved. The case is a "slice of life" that invites diagnosis, prescription and possible treatment. It may be presented in writing, orally, dramatically, on film, or as a recording.

Use the case method . . .

1. When relating a problem to life situations
2. When analyzing a problem
3. When members do not have ability to role play
4. To help members identify with a problem
5. When possible solutions are desired
6. When analyzing the bearing of facts upon a problem

Advantages	*Limitations*
1. May be written, filmed, recorded, acted out, or told as a story	1. Takes skill to "write" a problem out
2. May be assigned for study before discussion	2. Problem may not be equally relevant to all members
3. Provides equal opportunity for members to suggest solutions	3. Takes a great deal of time if done thoroughly
4. Creates the atmosphere for the exchange of ideas	4. Arguments tend to arise over whether the case presented enough facts
5. Deals with problems related to life	5. Requires skilled leadership
6. Provides opportunity to apply insights and skills	
7. Provides a type of simulated follow-through	

Brainstorming

Brainstorming is a method of problem solving in which group members suggest in rapid fire order all the possible solutions they can think of. Criticism is ruled out. Evaluation of ideas comes later.

Use the brainstorming method . . .

1. To encourage creative thinking
2. To encourage participation
3. When determining possible solutions to problems
4. In connection with other methods
5. To encourage presentation of new ideas
6. To create a warm, friendly feeling in the group

Advantages

1. Encourages new ideas
2. Encourages all members to take part
3. Produces a "chain reaction" of ideas
4. Does not take a great deal of time
5. Can be used with large or small groups
6. Does not require highly skilled leadership
7. Requires little equipment

Limitations

1. Can easily get out of hand
2. Evaluation must follow if method is to be effective
3. Members are slow to understand that *any* idea is acceptable
4. Members tend to begin evaluation when an idea is suggested

Listening teams

Listening teams are formed by dividing an audience into teams in advance of a presentation. Each team is requested to listen with specific assignments in mind. Teams then report on their assignment.

Use listening teams . . .

1. When important ideas may otherwise go unnoticed
2. When several sides of a problem need emphasis
3. When the group is large
4. To give purpose to discussion
5. To present information

Advantages

1. May be used with large or small groups
2. Pin-points certain ideas apart from the whole
3. Gives listener a specific purpose
4. Increases attention
5. Guides feedback
6. Creates interest
7. Permits all members to participate through listening
8. Encourages follow-up discussion
9. Lessens domination of discussion by one person or group
10. Gives leader opportunity to consider interests of group members
11. Provide for "repetition" through feedback

Limitations

1. Audience may "hear" only what is related to their assignment
2. Tends to detract from the whole
3. Limits exchange of ideas

The debate

Debate is a method in which speakers for and against a proposition present their points of view. Rebuttals may or may not follow. Instead of rebuttals, group members may question the debaters.

Use the debate method . . .

1. When issues need "sharpening"
2. To stimulate analysis
3. To present differing viewpoints
4. When members are willing to hear both sides of a question
5. When group is large

Advantages

1. Sharpens issues
2. Presents both sides of a question
3. Encourages analysis by group
4. Presents facts on both sides of an issue
5. Creates interest
6. Holds attention
7. Can be used with large groups

Limitations

1. Desire to "win" may be too strong
2. Members may get the wrong impression of the debaters
3. Limits group participation unless followed by discussion
4. May create too much emotional involvement
5. Requires a great deal of preparation

The formal discussion

Formal discussion is a systematic method of problem solving. It involves (1) stating the problem, (2) getting facts, (3) considering possible solutions, and (4) selecting best solutions.

Use formal discussion . . .

1. When sufficient time is available
2. When giving training in problem solving
3. To encourage logical thinking
4. When a problem is clearly defined
5. When a problem needs definition
6. To encourage thoroughness in solving problems
7. When the leader has sufficient skill to use the method
8. When the group is small enough for all to take part

Advantages	*Limitations*
1. Encourages logical thinking	1. Takes much time
2. Encourages thorough analysis	2. Requires skilled leadership
3. Procedure can be applied to variety of problems	3. Is difficult to use with large groups
4. Encourages high degree of concentration by group members	4. Requires a great deal of study on part of all members
5. Develops skill in identifying problems	5. May have to be extended over several discussion periods

The symposium (short speeches)

The symposium is a series of short speeches before an audience, with leadership; the speeches present different aspects of a topic.

Use the symposium method . . .

1. To present different aspects of a topic
2. When the group is large
3. When the group needs concise information
4. When qualified speakers are available
5. When no audience reaction is needed
6. When the subject matter is already determined

Advantages	*Limitations*
1. May be used with large or small groups	1. Lacks spontaneity and creativeness
2. May be used to present much information in a short time	2. Lacks group interaction
3. Spotlights issues	3. Emphasizes subject matter
4. Change of speakers increases interest and gives variety	4. Somewhat formal
5. May be planned completely ahead of time	5. Speakers' personalities can emphasize unduly the content
	6. Control of timing is difficult
	7. Limited in general to views of speakers
	8. Requires careful advance planning to insure adequate coverage
	9. Tends to be overused

The symposium-forum

The symposium-forum is a symposium followed by audience participation.

Use the symposium-forum method . . .

1. To provide for group interaction after a symposium
2. When a combination of content presentation and audience reaction is needed
3. When difficult ideas must be handled in the right way before they are openly discussed
4. When sufficient time and preparation are provided
5. When presenting different points of view for the purpose of audience reaction
6. When the group is large
7. When the group needs concise information

Advantages

1. Adds audience reaction to the values of the symposium
2. May be used with large or small groups (especially large groups)
3. Can be used to present much information in a short time
4. Spotlights issues
5. Change of speakers increases interest and adds variety
6. Audience reaction encourages purposeful listening

Limitations

1. Takes a lot of time
2. Group response is delayed
3. Speakers' personalities may emphasize content unduly
4. Control of timing is difficult
5. The forum period can easily get out of hand

Some Questions for You to Think About

1. How can a teacher or leader help a person discover what he needs or wants to learn? _____

_____

_____

2. Upon what does the effectiveness of methods depend?

_____

_____

3. How does the size of a group help determine the best method to use? _____

_____

_____

4. Which methods require the greatest skill on the part of the teacher or leader? _____

_____

_____

5. Which methods depend mainly upon the teacher or leader? _____

_____

_____

6. What is the difference between a panel and a symposium? _____

_____

_____

7. What is the difference between a panel and a panel-forum? _____

_____

_____

_____

8. Which methods encourage timid members to take part?

_____

_____

_____

9. Which methods could be used to follow brainstorming? Explain. _____

_____

_____

_____

10. What are some different ways to present a case study?

_____

_____

_____

11. What are some advantages and disadvantages of using listening teams during a session? role playing? debate? formal discussion? _____

_____

_____

_____

3. Use purposeful learning aids

(but remember—no learning aid is of itself either effective or ineffective)

The learning aid depends

   on the skill of the leader.

*The learning aid depends
on the size of the group.*

The learning aid also depends on . . .

PURPOSES

ABILITY OF PUPILS

FACILITIES

TIME AVAILABLE

COST

(This is a pinboard chart.)

Learning aids have many values . . .

(This is a slip chart.)

There are many kinds

of learning aids

from which to choose

Motion pictures

The motion picture is a "moving" picture, usually accompanied by sound.

USE MOTION PICTURES IN THESE WAYS

SHOW AN ENTIRE FILM TO BEGIN A STUDY

USE WITH A DISCUSSION METHOD

SHOW AS A PREVIEW OR REVIEW OF A STUDY

STOP THE FILM FOR DISCUSSION

ASK LISTENING TEAMS TO LISTEN FOR IDEAS

(This is a folded word strip chart.)

Use motion pictures . . .

1. To secure emotional involvement
2. When equipment is available
3. To present sounds and scenes realistically
4. To shorten time needed for training
5. To attract and hold attention
6. To create interest
7. To deepen impressions
8. To increase retention
9. To provide variety in learning experiences
10. To make learning uniform

Advantages	*Limitations*
1. Approach real life experiences	1. Films may not be available
2. Appeal to emotions	2. Cost may be too high
3. Show motion, timing, phasing	3. Equipment may not be available
4. Assure consistency of presentation with teachers of varying ability	4. Require trained operators
5. May be used in many ways—by showing all or parts of films	5. Require darkened rooms
6. Make use of sight and sound	6. Most films are too long for use with group discussions

Film strips

A film strip is a series of still pictures designed to be projected on a screen or other surface.

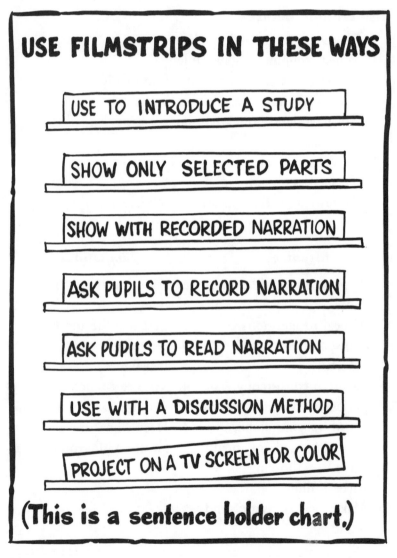

USE FILMSTRIPS IN THESE WAYS

USE TO INTRODUCE A STUDY

SHOW ONLY SELECTED PARTS

SHOW WITH RECORDED NARRATION

ASK PUPILS TO RECORD NARRATION

ASK PUPILS TO READ NARRATION

USE WITH A DISCUSSION METHOD

PROJECT ON A TV SCREEN FOR COLOR

(This is a sentence holder chart.)

Use film strips . . .

1. To attract and hold attention
2. To create interest
3. To deepen impressions
4. To increase retention
5. To provide variety in learning experiences
6. To shorten time needed for training
7. When pictorial realism is important
8. When equipment is available

Advantages

1. Lower in cost than motion pictures
2. Fairly easy to use
3. All or parts may be used
4. Combines sight and sound
5. May be purchased because of low cost
6. May be used over and over
7. May be used with groups of all sizes
8. May be used in many ways
9. May be presented in a short time
10. Require less darkening of room than motion pictures

Limitations

1. Not as dramatic as motion pictures
2. Require trained operators
3. Equipment may not be available
4. Require previewing
5. Leaders tend to "show" instead of use
6. Teachers sometimes use as a crutch or substitute for preparation
7. Require time for setting up equipment

Charts

A chart is a visual symbol which presents an idea and explains it.

(This is a wantad flipchart.)

Use charts . . .

1. To attract and hold attention
2. To develop an idea
3. When presenting information
4. When pupils can read
5. When budget is limited
6. When the group is small
7. To time a presentation·
8. When a permanent record is needed
9. To review and preview
10. To highlight key points
11. To add variety to discussion methods
12. To speed up learning
13. To increase retention

Advantages

1. Attract attention
2. May be prepared in advance
3. Cost very little
4. May be used in many ways
5. Provide permanent record
6. May be used repeatedly
7. Notes may be written on edge of sheets
8. May be prepared from readily available materials

Limitations

1. Cannot be used with large groups
2. Less flexible to use than the chalkboard
3. Require time for preparation
4. Require some skill in preparation

Kinds of charts

PINBOARD CHART

(Word strips rest on pins stuck in a backing.)

G.A.'S — pins or tacks
Y.W.A.
SUNBEAMS — word strips

SENTENCE HOLDER CHART

(Word strips rest in shallow pocket.)

SHORT TALKS
PANEL — pockets
ROLE PLAY — word strips

HINGED CHART

(Word strips are hinged so they may be flipped down.)

HINGED CHART — flip down word strips
— tape hinges

FOLDED WORD STRIP CHART

(Word strips are folded in the center, then opened.)

FOLDED WORD STRIP — folded word strips

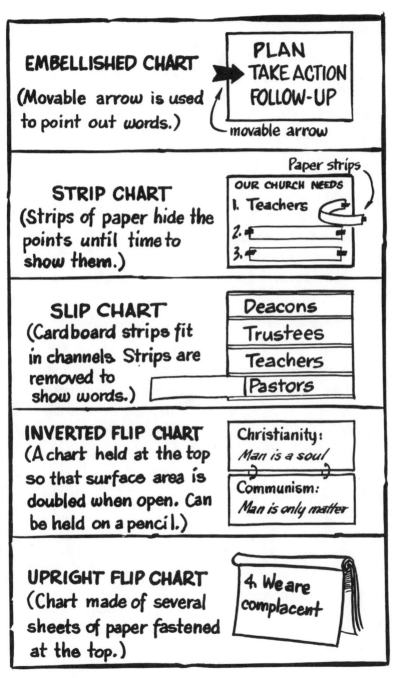

EMBELLISHED CHART
(Movable arrow is used to point out words.)

PLAN
TAKE ACTION
FOLLOW-UP
— movable arrow

STRIP CHART
(Strips of paper hide the points until time to show them.)

Paper strips
OUR CHURCH NEEDS
1. Teachers
2.
3.

SLIP CHART
(Cardboard strips fit in channels. Strips are removed to show words.)

Deacons
Trustees
Teachers
Pastors

INVERTED FLIP CHART
(A chart held at the top so that surface area is doubled when open. Can be held on a pencil.)

Christianity:
Man is a soul

Communism:
Man is only matter

UPRIGHT FLIP CHART
(Chart made of several sheets of paper fastened at the top.)

4. We are complacent

Maps

A map is a representation, usually on a flat surface, of the surface of the earth, or some part of it.

Use maps . . .
1. To add "believability" to a presentation
2. To show relative position and size of places
3. To attract and hold attention
4. To add interest to a presentation
5. To increase retention
6. To speed up learning
7. To secure learner response
8. To help in planning a route

Advantages	*Limitations*
1. Cost very little	1. May get out of date
2. May be handled easily	2. Easily misplaced unless permanently mounted
3. May be used in a variety of ways	3. May not be available
4. May be used by learners as well as leaders	4. Most leaders have not learned to use maps creatively
5. May be used repeatedly	
6. Add "believability"	
7. Attract and hold attention	
8. Deepen interest	
9. Increase retention	
10. Speed up learning	

Kinds of maps

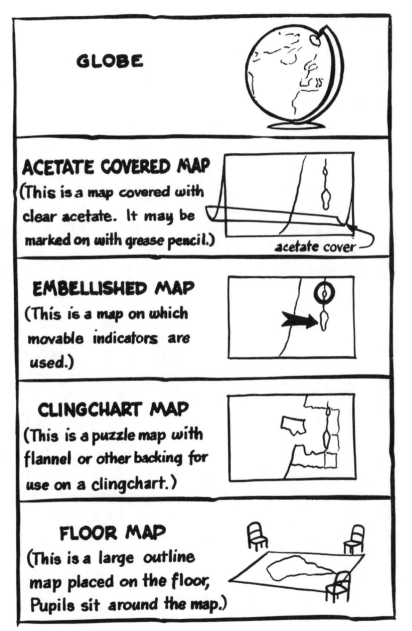

GLOBE

ACETATE COVERED MAP
(This is a map covered with clear acetate. It may be marked on with grease pencil.)

acetate cover

EMBELLISHED MAP
(This is a map on which movable indicators are used.)

CLINGCHART MAP
(This is a puzzle map with flannel or other backing for use on a clingchart.)

FLOOR MAP
(This is a large outline map placed on the floor, Pupils sit around the map.)

Chalkboards

A chalkboard is a writing surface especially treated for use with chalk.

Use chalkboards...

1. *Often*—they are the "work horses" of learning aids
2. When the group or class is recording ideas
3. When material does not need to be permanently recorded
4. When making an outline for a single session
5. To secure learner participation
6. To attract and hold attention
7. To add interest to a presentation
8. To increase retention
9. To speed up learning

Advantages

1. Cost very little
2. Are usually available
3. May be used in a variety of ways
4. May be changed during a presentation
5. Are simple to use
6. Attract and hold attention
7. Deepen interest
8. Increase retention
9. Speed up learning
10. May be used to secure learner participation

Limitations

1. Do not provide a permanent record
2. May become commonplace
3. Are usually stationary
4. Cannot be used with large groups
5. Most leaders have not learned to use chalkboards creatively

Ways to use the chalkboard

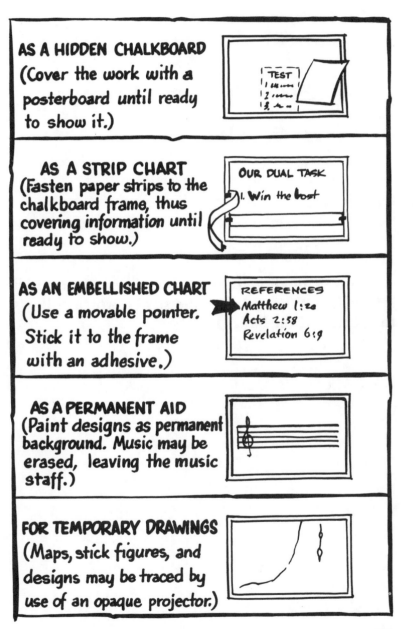

AS A HIDDEN CHALKBOARD
(Cover the work with a posterboard until ready to show it.)

AS A STRIP CHART
(Fasten paper strips to the chalkboard frame, thus covering information until ready to show.)

AS AN EMBELLISHED CHART
(Use a movable pointer. Stick it to the frame with an adhesive.)

AS A PERMANENT AID
(Paint designs as permanent background. Music may be erased, leaving the music staff.)

FOR TEMPORARY DRAWINGS
(Maps, stick figures, and designs may be traced by use of an opaque projector.)

4. Plan follow-through activities

(Follow-through is a means of pursuing an initial effort. It is "that part of the stroke which follows the hitting of the ball.")

Follow-through can be

an individual activity . . .

... like reading a book

Follow-through can be
a group activity . . .

Follow-through is

   important . . .

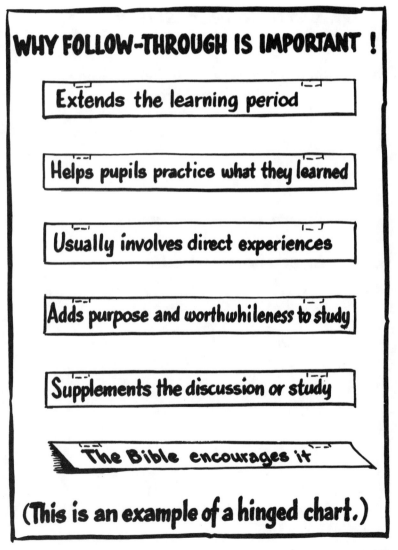

WHY FOLLOW-THROUGH IS IMPORTANT !

Extends the learning period

Helps pupils practice what they learned

Usually involves direct experiences

Adds purpose and worthwhileness to study

Supplements the discussion or study

The Bible encourages it

(This is an example of a hinged chart.)

5. Evaluate results

(Evaluation is a "stock take" to help us know where to go from here.)

There are many ways

to evaluate results.

Some evaluation methods . . .

TESTING

Give a test.

WRITING A NARRATIVE

Ask learner to write what he has learned.

KEEPING A CONVERSATION FLOW CHART

Show how often and to whom pupils spoke.

Attendance Last Week	180
Attendance Today	181
Number Absent	96

COUNTING

Count or "take a show of hands."

(check one)
This helped me

☐ More
☐ Less

than the study last week.

CHECKING OPINION SHEETS

Ask pupils to express their opinions on a ballot.

OBSERVING

Ask an observer to report what he observed.

Evaluation may relate to . . .

... the study materials

QUAR-
TERLY

Studies
in
Acts

... the procedures
or methods

... the product

The teacher should evaluate them all.

Some Questions for You to Think About

1. What are some values of using learning aids?
   _____
   _____
   _____

2. What are some of the different types of charts?
   _____
   _____
   _____

3. When is it best to use motion pictures? filmstrips?
   _____
   _____
   _____

4. What are some ways to use maps in teaching? How can
   a teacher or leader let pupils help in the use of maps?
   _____
   _____
   _____

5. What are some advantages and disadvantages of using
   charts? chalkboards? _____
   _____
   _____

6. What are six reasons why follow-through activities are
   important? _____
   _____
   _____

7. What are six different methods for evaluating learning?
   _____
   _____
   _____

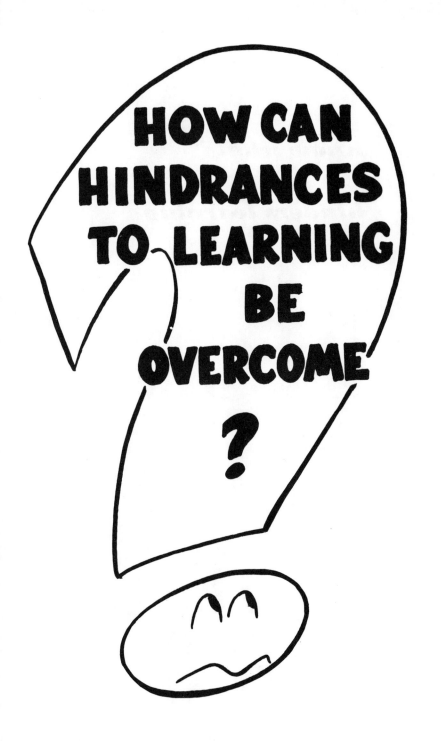

Know what

hinders learning

Sometimes the place is . . .

Sometimes the place is . . .

...too large

Sometimes the place is . . .

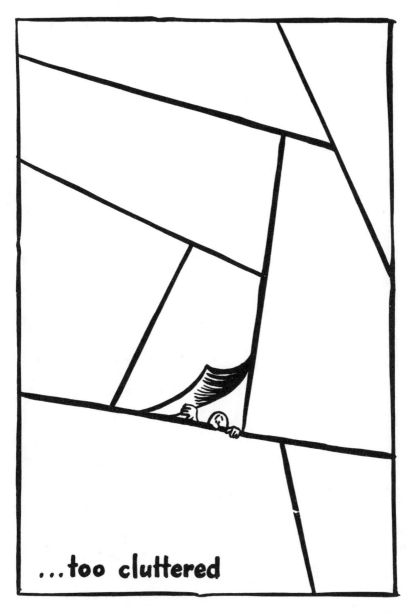

...too cluttered

Sometimes the place is . . .

...too stuffy

Sometimes the group is too large.

(This chart shows *person-to-person* relationships only. The number of relationships of *all kinds* increases 127 per cent each time one person is added to a group!)

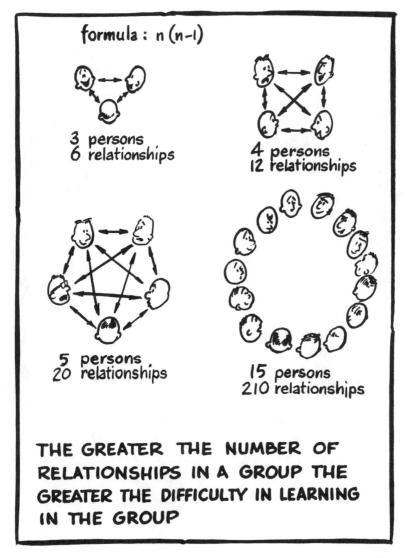

formula : n (n-1)

3 persons
6 relationships

4 persons
12 relationships

5 persons
20 relationships

15 persons
210 relationships

THE GREATER THE NUMBER OF RELATIONSHIPS IN A GROUP THE GREATER THE DIFFICULTY IN LEARNING IN THE GROUP

The differing attitudes of group members make learning difficult.

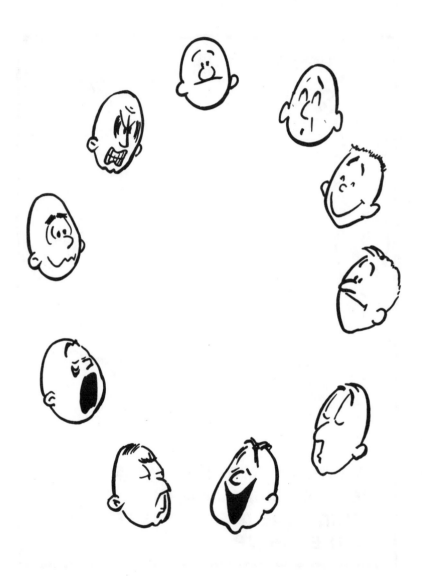

Some group members get upset
when others disagree with them.

ALL NOT IN FAVOR, SAY, "I QUIT!"

*Some group members don't feel free
to say what they think.*

Some group members

feel out of place.

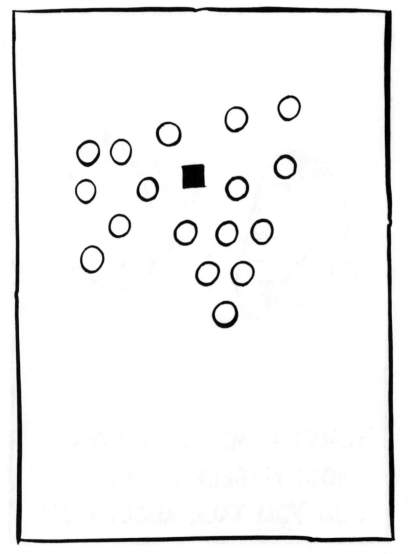

Some group members
are self-centered.

Work to overcome

the hindrances

to learning

You could remove

all hindrances by . . .

Respect opinions.

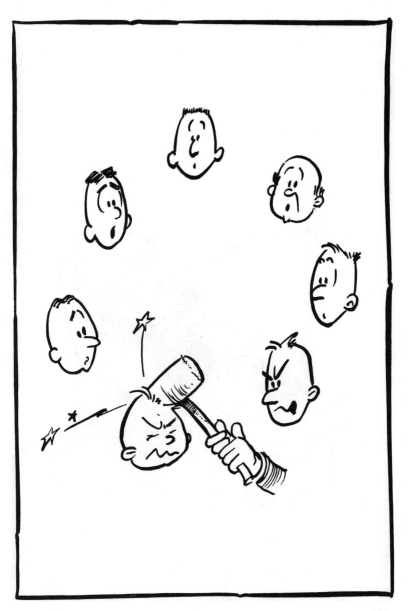

Provide a comfortable place.

Use first names.

Let the group members talk, too!

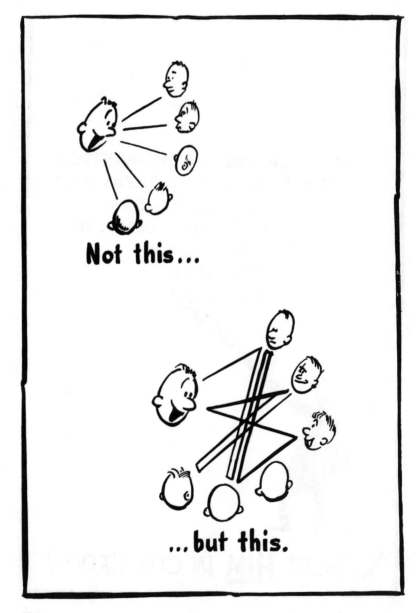

Not this...

...but this.

Some Questions for You to Think About

1. What are some factors which hinder learning?

   _____

   _____

   _____

2. What are some factors (other than those mentioned in this book) which hinder learning? _____

   _____

   _____

   _____

3. When is a group too large for effective learning?

   _____

   _____

   _____

4. How many person-to-person relationships exist in groups consisting of the following numbers of persons? The mathematical formula n(n-1) may be used in determining answers. _____

   50 persons_____ 75 persons_____

    8 persons_____ 34 persons_____

5. What can a teacher or leader do to help group members feel free to express their own opinions? _____

   _____

   _____

   _____

6. In the spaces below write one-word descriptions of the attitudes suggested by the "faces" on page 126.

   _____ _____

   _____ _____

   _____ _____

   _____ _____

What this book has said.

This book has made use of pictures and words to help teachers and leaders answer these important questions:

1. Who *is* the learner?

The learner is himself! He is different from every other person in age, appearance, ability to learn, and talents. He is different in likes and dislikes, background and experience, and in many other ways.

The learner's differences affect the way he learns. Teachers and leaders must consider these differences in determining what to teach and how to teach. These differences help the teacher know whether to teach to improve the learner's skills, change his attitudes, or to increase his knowledge.

2. How does the learner learn?

He learns through his experiences. Many, but not all, of his experiences come through his senses. He has five senses —sight, hearing, smell, taste, and touch. Learning is usually better when the learner uses more than one sense at the same time. The good teacher or leader remembers, however, that not all experiences can be accounted for through the senses.

There are many kinds of experiences. Some are real life experiences—like hitting a thumb with a hammer or going on a trip. Some are direct but "made-up" or "play-like" experiences—such as acting in a play. Some experiences are indirect, using words or other symbols—such as reading a book or listening to a speech. Some experiences are indirect, using representations of real things—such as seeing a film or picture. Direct experiences use more senses than indirect experiences.

3. Which experiences are "best" for the learner?

No *one* type of experience is always best. The learner's differences determine the kinds of experiences which are best for him. When the learner has had many real life experiences, it is easier for him to learn from indirect experiences. Generally, the older and more experienced the learner, the fewer direct experiences he must have.

Direct experiences take much more time than indirect experiences. It is impossible for one to learn all he needs to from direct experiences. Indirect experiences can speed up learning.

4. How can learning be improved?

Learning can be improved by helping the learner discover what he wants or needs to learn. The teacher or leader can challenge the learner with a problem, ask him to write down what he wants to learn, or ask him what his problem is. The teacher or leader may find out whether the lesson fits the learner's needs. Giving a test is one of the best ways to find out what the learner needs to learn.

Learning can be improved by use of good methods. But no method is of itself effective or ineffective. The method depends upon the purposes, abilities of the leader and learner, the size of the group, the time available, the facilities, and many other factors.

There are many methods from which to choose. These include the lecture, group discussion, panel, panel-forum, small study groups, role playing, case study, brainstorming, symposium, symposium-forum, listening teams, debate, formal discussion, and many others. All of these methods have advantages and limitations. The earnest teacher or leader will learn when and where to use them.

Learning can be improved by use of purposeful learning aids. No learning aid is of itself either effective or ineffective. The learning aid depends on the skill of the leader, the size of the group, the purposes, ability of learners, facilities, time available—and cost.

Learning aids have many values. They attract and hold attention, help time a presentation, increase retention, speed up learning, and create anticipation.

There are many kinds of learning aids from which to choose. Some of the kinds of learning aids are the motion picture, film strips, charts, maps, and chalkboards. All of them have advantages and limitations. The teacher or leader should know these advantages and limitations. He should gain skill in using the aids and in knowing when and where to use them.

Learning can be improved by planning for follow-through. Follow-through is a means of pursuing or continuing an initial effort. It is "that part of the stroke which follows the striking of the ball."

Follow-through can be an individual activity—like reading a book. It can be a group activity—like going on a picnic. Follow-through activities extend the learning period, help learners practice what they have learned, and add purpose to the study. Follow-through makes repetition possible. Repetition increases the effectiveness of learning.

Learning can be improved by evaluating results of study. Evaluation is a "stock take" to help the teacher or leader know "where to go from here."

There are many ways to evaluate results. Some of these methods are testing, writing a narrative or story, keeping a conversation flow chart, counting, checking opinion sheets, or asking a person to observe and report.

Study materials, methods, and the product may be evaluated. The product is the most difficult to evaluate, especially when it is a change in attitude. Changes in skills and knowledge are more easily measured than changes in attitudes. Attitudes are desirable by-products of learning activities.

5. How can hindrances to learning be overcome?

Many experiences and much learning take place in groups. Group members teach one another and learn from one another. Sometimes learning in groups is difficult.

Hindrances to learning can be overcome by knowing the things which hinder learning. Sometimes the place is too small or too large or too cluttered. Sometimes the air is too stuffy. Sometimes the group is too large. Differing attitudes sometimes made learning difficult. Some people get upset when others disagree with them. Some group members don't feel free to say what they think. They feel out of place. Some people are self-centered. But these difficulties can be overcome to some extent.

Hindrances to learning can be overcome when the teacher or leader works hard to overcome them. Of course, he could remove all the hindrances by removing all the people! But there are better ways. The teacher or leader can respect opinions, provide a comfortable place, use first names, let the pupils or learners do some of the talking, and take the steps necessary for effective learning.

By finding out what a learner needs and how he learns, a teacher or leader can know what to teach and how to teach. To this end these pictures and words have been brought together in this book.